NiGHt LIGhTs

24 Poems To Sleep On

DENYS CAZET

ORCHARD BOOKS

NEW YORK

Orchard Books
95 Madison Avenue
New York, NY 10016

Manufactured in the United States of America
Printed by Barton Press, Inc.
Bound by Horowitz/Rae
Book design by Jennifer Campbell

10 9 8 7 6 5 4 3 2 1

The text of this book is set in 15 point Simoncini Garamond.
The illustrations are pencil and watercolor.

Library of Congress Cataloging-in-Publication Data
Cazet, Denys.
Night lights : 24 poems to sleep on / Denys Cazet.
p.   cm.
Summary: A collection of poems, both silly and soothing, that
focus on bedtime, such as "Good-night Kisses," "How to Humiliate
the Boogeyman," and "Where Am I When I Dream?"
ISBN 0-531-30010-2. — ISBN 0-531-33010-9 (lib. bdg.)
1. Children's poetry, American. 2. Bedtime—Juvenile poetry.
[1. Bedtime—Poetry. 2. American poetry.] I. Title.
PS3553.A99N54 1997 811'.54—dc20 96-42282

There was an old grandpa
who lived in the flue.
He had so many grandchildren
he didn't know what to do.
So he wrote them a book
with a silver quill-pen,
then put them to bed
 and told them to read it
  again
   and again
    and again
     and again
      and . . .

Nick, Max,
where are you?
Ty, Kasey,
Jonathan,
I know you're
in here
somewhere.
Time to read.

Night Lights

The sea has the lighthouse,
watching afar.
The earth has the moon,
and heaven a star.

Our house has the porch light,
so you can see.
What more could I ask for?
Mama's with me.

Some sheep
leap.

Not Afraid of the Dark

I don't really need a night light,
I don't care what my sister said,
I'm not afraid of the dark,
I LIKE a searchlight near the bed.

My sister says the light's excessive,
but I need the light to read,
and it's mighty handy for spotting
the creeping centipede.

It keeps away the Boogerman,
and the Nipping-Nincompoop.
It keeps away the hungry ghoul
that wants me for his soup.

It keeps away the shadows
where the creepies like to dwell,
like the poison macaroon
and the flying mackerel.

It keeps away the biting ogre
and the stinging purple blister.
But most of all it's mighty handy
for keeping away my sister.

And some . . .

Good-night Kisses

"Time to go to bed," my mama said.
"Time to kiss everyone good-night."
And so, I KISSED . . .

nine sisters, eight brothers,
a cousin or two,
Uncle Fester, Aunt Minnie,
and Mister Magoo.
My dog and her puppies,
our cat and her fleas,
all the mice in the basement
and a pound of blue cheese.
The hamster, the gerbil,
the tropical fish,
a gushy persimmon
in Mama's blue dish.
Grandpa and Grandma,
Aunt Mildred's new wig,
the carpet, the sofa,
and Porkus the Pig.
Mama and Papa,
I almost forgot,
an onion, the broccoli,
a lonely shallot.
The doors and the windows,
the books on the shelf—
I think I'll bend over
and kiss my sweet self.

"That should do it!" my mama said.
"Now give us a hug . . . and go to bed."
AND SO . . .

*Time to
say
good-night.*

Nocturnal Concert

Many play the piano, some play the bassoon,
but I play the schnozzola, my brother the spoon.
Together, once Papa has fallen fast asleep,
across the bedroom floor silently we creep.
Patiently we wait until we hear the snores,
and then we begin with the wheezes and the roars.

While my brother raps the rhythm upon Papa's pate,
I fine-tune the schnozzola until the snores abate.
I finger the nostrils, I gently pinch the nose,
and then we play a rendition of "My Wild Irish Rose."

Grandpa Said

The Murphy bed lies in wait,
hidden in the wall,
waiting to open its monstrous mouth,
to consume me . . . all in all.

My grandpa says I'm right,
he slept there once, he knows,
it swallowed him, then spit him out,
'cause he hadn't washed his toes.

Uncle Willie slept there too!
That's what my grandpa said,
and in the morning, when Willie woke,
he woke without a head.

Grandma says don't listen.
Please . . . go brush your teeth.
But I know how much Grandpa loves me:
he said he'd leave a wreath.

Nobody ever listens to me.

Where Does the Moon Go When It Shrinks?

I've been wondering, I've been thinking,
since very early June,
about the complexity of the cosmos,
about the shrinking of the moon.

I asked my father to explain it.
He's the smartest man alive.
I know because he told me
in his direction I should strive.

He was silent for a moment,
nodding gravely so.
Suddenly he shouted,
"Here's what you need to know.

"The moon is nothing but a wad of cheap caulking compound that's stuffed in a black hole to keep all the stars from leaking out. So, if you don't wire-brush all your surfaces, it's going to leak, you know, like maybe every twenty-nine days or something. You gotta watch it. We're not talking about your common soldered joint. I mean, you got a leak here—we're talking major. You get your galactic bowl jammed and you can't just call up some cosmic rooter service. Finding a good plumber isn't easy. You know what I mean?

"Science is amazing, isn't it? Never be afraid to ask me a question, son ... no matter how silly you think your question might be! Thanks for asking. Sleep tight."

The Plumber's Guide to the Universe?

I pulled up the covers
and turned off the light,
thinking and thinking
for most of the night.

I'm grateful he's helpful—
to me, my sisters, my brother—
but if I have any more questions
I think I'll ask my mother.

Can't She Take a Joke!?

I have a message from your sisssster.

SUNDAY
I stuffed some frogs in my sister's bed.
She nearly had a stroke.
"I'll pay you back," she screamed at me.
Can't she take a joke!?

MONDAY
I quickly slipped beneath the covers,
barely half-awake,
until I heard the coiled hissssss
of my sister's snake.

TUESDAY
I snuck into my sister's room,
snickering at my grand design:
between her clean and perfumed sheets
I tucked a porcupine.

WEDNESDAY
when I went to bed, I thought I'd won.
There was no muss or fuss
until I fluffed and punched my pillow:
it was an octopus.

*Pssst . . . pssst . . .
excuse me . . . have
you tried* eau de skunk?

THURSDAY
my sister had a heavy date
(she was in love with Mr. Hunk)
so . . . she took a little beauty rest
and found a little skunk.

FRIDAY
I poked my bed with a curtain rod
to see what it might conceal.
Imagine my shock and stunned surprise
to find an electric eel.

SATURDAY
our parents said, "Enough's enough!
We demand a sibling truce."
Oh, sure, I thought, easy to say, so
where do I put the moose?

I Must Have a Bed of My Own

Mama, Papa, I beg you, please,
I'm not a baby, I'm almost grown,
I'm tired of sharing.
Please . . . can't I have a bed of my own?

When you roll over
and I'm squashed in the middle,
I feel like a waffle
stuck in the griddle.

And when Papa is dreaming
and he trumpets the night,
it's as though someone woke me—
with dynamite.

And what could be worse
than elephant musk?
I'll tell you . . . getting poked in the night
by an elephant tusk!

Mama, Papa, I beg you, please,
can't I sleep alone?
I must have a place, my very own space.
Please . . . I must have a bed of my own.

*See
what I
mean?*

How To Humiliate the Boogeyman

(Sing this song in your bed)

Hey! Hey!
Mr. Halibut Head.
HEY! HEY!
Get away from my bed.
You heard what I said—
Get away from the bed.
HEY! HEY!
Mr. Stinky Fish Head.

Did you hear what I said,
Mr. Halibut Head?
Try and scare me, see if you can;
Go ahead, try,
You'll probably cry,
Mr. Boogey the Boo-hoo Boohooman.

Mr. Make-Believe Sham,
Mr. Flash-in-the-Pan,
Your complexion's a pale pea green;
The eyes on your face
Are all over the place,
You are the ugliest thing never seen.

Mr. Fake, Mr. Phony,
Mr. Full-of-Baloney,
Decked out in green bombazine;
With a nose like a yam,
You have the brains of a clam,
And you smell like a dead sardine.

So give it a rest,
Mr. Boogeyman pest,
And get away from the foot of my bed—
Or I'll turn on the light.
Hey! Hey! Good-night,
Toodle-oo, Mr. Halibut Head.

And then she called me Halibut Head and Mr. Stinky and now my self-esteem is down the drain—and there goes my job too! And then . . .

Is this guy a big doofus— or what?

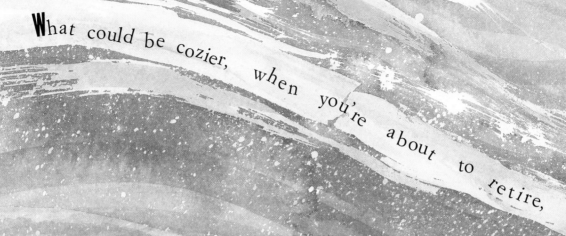

What could be cozier, when you're about to retire,

Inside, Outside

Me out,
Me out,
Me out.

Meow,
Meow,
Meow.

Meow, Meow, Meow.

Meowt,
Meowt,
Meowt.

than bunny pajamas right out of the dryer?

Go Where?

My father said to go to sleep,
but . . . I don't see it on this map.
How am I supposed to go there
if I don't know where it's at?

Boris Can't Sleep

Pajama attired, poor Boris was tired,
hadn't slept a wink in a week.
He rang up his doctor and pleaded for sleep.
The doctor's suggestion was simple. "Boris," he said.
"Try counting something. . . . Try counting sheep!"

So he slipped away, without delay,
and embarked on his wolfish ways.
He played the recorder, crossing the border,
and then snatched a bundle of sheep. "There!" he said.
"That's exactly what the doctor ordered."

Hoping for slumber, he gave each a number,
then led them in a chorus of song,
and when they were done, the last lullaby sung,
Boris blessed them with a sprinkle of salt. "Okay," he said.
"The time has come. Let us start with number one."

And so, one by one, until he was done,
Boris followed the doctor's prescription.
He numerically dined on a hundred and nine
varieties of mulligan mutton. "It works," he yawned.
"I'm exhausted.... Tomorrow ... I'll try counting swine."

Midnight Snack

Beneath
the midnight moon
a sleepy little crocodile
yawned,
drifting down the Nile.

He listened to the night,
he sighed a sleepy sigh,
he listened to the river
as a froggy drifted by.

WHAP! SNAP!
GOOD-BYE, FROGGY!
MIDNIGHT SNACK!

He felt a little sleepier,
he sighed a sleepy sigh,
he listened to the river
as a piggy drifted by.

WHAP! SNAP!
GOOD-BYE, PIGGY!
MIDNIGHT SNACK!

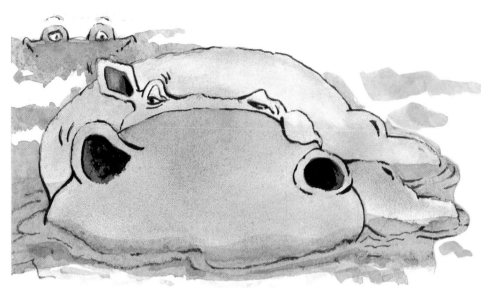

He felt a little sleepier,
he sighed a sleepy sigh,
he listened to the river
as a hippo drifted by.

WHAP! SNAP!
GOOD-BYE, HIPPO!
MIDNIGHT SNACK!

Beneath
the midnight moon
an enormous crocodile
slept,
drifting down the Nile.

The Day I Was Sick I Had a Dream

I had a dream
of a thunderous cough
that exploded my nose
and blew my ears off.

My eyes flew out,
ricocheted off the floor,
bounced about,
and stuck to the door.

Mom asked the doctor,
"What should we do?"
"No problem," he uttered.
"I think it's the flu."

The Sandman

My grandpa said,
"Young man, you should wear a hat
and strap these goggles to your head.

"That way, when the Sandman tries
to send you to slumberland,
he can't throw any sand in your eyes.

"You can lie back on your bed
and say, 'Nice try, Bozo, but I'm wearing goggles.'
Then you can stay awake instead."

The Dream of Gertrude Holstein

One soft and lazy summer night,
Gertrude had a dream.
She dreamt she was a pole vaulter
on the Olympic team.

The crowd was hushed, the score was tied,
Gertrude was the last.
It was up to her, now or never.
The crowd stood up, aghast.

Gertrude Holstein stood alone, ready,
waiting for the starting gun.
How would history remember her
when all was said and done?

The gun roared out a monstrous BANG,
a thunderous thunderclap
that sent Gertrude Holstein, a locomotive,
steaming down the track.

She rammed the pole with bovine fury.
At exactly ten past noon,
Gertrude hurtled herself skyward
and whirled past the moon.

And then, as if by magic, she flew,
drifting through the clouds,
and landed as gently as a dove
to the roaring of the crowd.

The cheering faded to a murmur
as Gertrude stretched and stirred,
waking to the morning sounds
of a chatty mockingbird.

"Mock me if you must," she yawned,
"but . . . this dream divine,
this gold medal dream, this dream of dreams,
will be forever mine."

I've Never Seen My Goldfish Sleep

Even though I've watched for hours,
I've never seen my goldfish blink,
I've never seen her close her eyes,
Never seen her wink.

What's she watching? What's she see?
What's she staring at?
It must be something. . . . Is it me?
Is she watching for the cat?

What's she thinking? Is she sad?
Can a goldfish have the blues?
Does she nap? Does she slumber?
Does she ever snooze?

What flights of fancy does she dream?
What secrets does she keep?
What urges her to stay awake
And never, never sleep?

The Snail's Dream

Awake,
the snail
moves
very,
very,
very
slowly.

But in her dream,
she moves
a teensy,
weensy,
itsy,
bitsy,
teeny,
weeny
bit
faster.

My Brother Is a Fuddy-duddy

My little brother is two.

When he goes to bed,
he closes the door, just so,
gathers his favorite books,
turns on his record player,
plays "Peter Pan,"
second side only,
rummages around in his closet,
finds a stuffed toy,
and then climbs into Mom's lap.
She reads all of his books.
Then he gets down,
turns off the light,
climbs back into Mom's lap,
and they rock for twenty minutes.
Then he slides off her lap,
climbs into his crib by himself—
he won't let you help him—
and Mom has to cover him up
between his two favorite blankets.
He looks like a baby sandwich.
And then—you won't believe this—
he has to kiss Mom first,
and say, "Sweet dreams,"
because if she says it first,
he makes a big fuss.
He's such a fuddy-duddy.
Like it really matters,
you know what I mean?

I am six.
I am in kindergarten.

When I go to bed,
I require nothing more than
a glass of warm milk by the lamp,
fresh flowers, and a massage.

Where Am I When I Dream?

Where am I when I dream?
Am I here,
Safely nestled in my bed,
Or am I there,
Within the dream,
Elsewhere, elsewhere.

And how is it that my mother
Is always so aware
Of where I am
And when I am
Trapped there,
Having left the things I know,
Crying in the nightmare place,
And then, there she is,
And here I am,
Wrapped in her warm embrace.

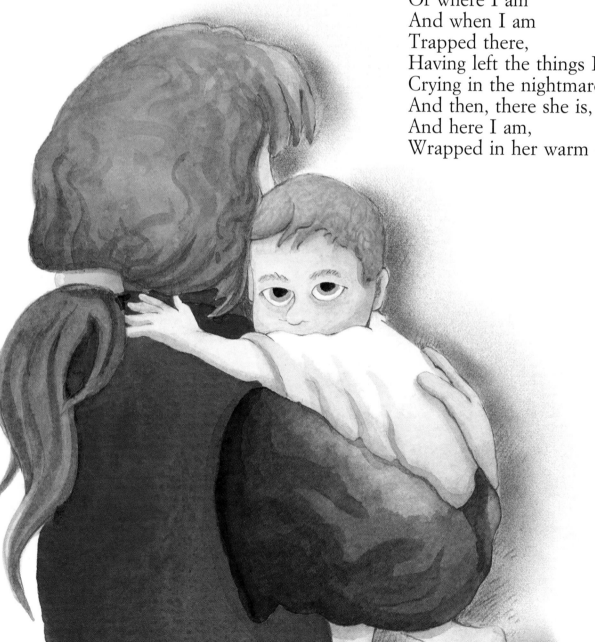

The Song Has Begun

Listen, my son, the song has begun,
listen to the psalm of the night.
Snug in your blanket, your Superman cloak,
Papa will rock you to sleep.

The Man in the Moon sings you a tune,
wrapped in a Milky Way ribbon.
The wind in the trees, a chorus of leaves
singing "Sweet dreams" at the window.

Papa is here, Mama is near,
Brown Bear is already asleep.
Listen, my son, the song has begun,
Papa will rock you to sleep.

I Have a Dream Waiting

You might be wondering why
I'm skipping to my bed.
It's because I have a dream
stirring in my head.

A just-for-me dream
waiting in the twilight,
waiting with the silent stars,
calling in the night.

So if you don't mind, tuck me in,
give me a kiss, and off with the light.
I have a dream waiting. . . .
Good-night.